TIMOTHY GAGER
2 0 2 0 POEMS

2020 Poems © 2021 Timothy Gager. All rights reserved. Big Table Publishing Company retains the right to reprint. Permission to reprint must be obtained from the author, who owns the copyright.

ISBN: 978-1-945917-65-3

Printed in the United States of America

Cover Design: Matt Siditsky
Additional Editing: Sarah Gordon

Also by Timothy Gager:

Spreading Like Wild Flowers
Grand Slams: A Coming of Eggs Story
The Thursday Appointments of Bill Sloan
The Shutting Door
Treating A Sick Animal: Flash and Micro Fictions

Some of these poems have appeared previously:

"New York Confession"- *Live Nude Poems*
"When You Have This Connection", "How Lucia Joyce Was Treated", "Midwinter Aficionado", "Thinking In Long Distant Relations", "April 27, 2020" - *Muddy River Poetry Review*
"Kleptoparasitic" - *Boston Literary Magazine*
"Existential Crisis" - *Broadkill Review*
"Spin the Bottle" – *Bagel Bards Anthology*

"Making other books jealous since 2004"

Big Table Publishing Company
Boston, MA and San Francisco, CA
www.bigtablepublishing.com

Introduction
Ten Years Since Life Started: November 6, 2010

Ten—a big round number for my sobriety. When my journey started, I didn't think I could go a day, a week, a month and certainly not a year. Alcohol and drugs were all the life I knew. Now, I know life differently. I can get through today, get to midnight, and do it again without the physical and mental dependence on a substance.

Generally, 2020 was not an easy year for people in sobriety. It certainly wasn't an easy year for me. In July of 2019, my mom was diagnosed with cancer. One week later, when I celebrated my ninth anniversary of sobriety, she went for a cancer treatment and fell upon entering her ride there. Unable to stand, she went to the ER instead of Dana Farber Cancer Institute, where they ran tests and admitted her to South Shore Hospital. She was moved to hospice care shortly after, and would never go home again. She died on Christmas night. Gratefully, I could wake up on December 26 still sober.

After her passing, my father's condition decompensated at a quick rate. My mother and father had been married for over 65 years. They relied on each other and each picked up the slack in the skills the other lacked. Before being hospitalized, my mother had been caring more and more for my father as his short term memory had begun to falter a bit. My brother and sisters and I knew he would not be able to live independently anymore. He decided to move to Maryland, into an assisted-living facility close to my brother Fred and his family.

Then, the pandemic. My dad left Massachusetts in late February just before Covid-19 restrictions hit. By March, visitation at his new place was no longer allowed, and my brother and his family generously took him into their home "temporarily" until restrictions were eased. As of November 2020, he is still living there, and his symptoms have worsened. My brilliant father, an engineering genius who worked on radar defense systems for the government, is losing much of his cognitive ability. To say that my family has lost my father as well as my mother in the past year is a fair and painful assessment. I miss both of them every day. Some days are fine, but as the seasons move to autumn, they trigger emotions: memories of seeing my mom in hospice daily, and spending that extra time with dad—the opportunity of which I no longer have.

Lately, the days are difficult. I am sorry that my brother, sister-in-law, nieces, and nephews will have new and upsetting memories of my father not being the man they knew. Still, I find strength and faith through the work I've done in the last ten years not to have a drink over any of this.

In the world outside of mine, I didn't drink over our divided country, especially in terms of the dishonesty we are shown and have come to expect as citizens. We have taken backwards steps regarding racial justice, women's rights, and support for LBGTQIA+ community. We have forgone a healthy and safe earth—and made Twitter feeds or conspiracies more important than science. From the top down, we are rotting as if we are in a vegetable drawer that is stuck closed.

In 2020, loved ones got sick and died, and communities shut down for safety. Many jobs and businesses failed because of Covid-19. I began to work from home and left my house just a few times per week. I am still living without much human contact, but have been able to adapt because of who I have become. I am lucky to have a special person in my life, and we try to see each other once per week. She has encouraged me to re-start my Dire Literary Series as a Zoom event, and to play guitar again. We even have band practice—all play, and no work. Being sober has allowed me to have all of this.

As for virtual life, Zoom has been a wonderful tool. It allows me to attend meetings to maintain my sobriety, and to attend meetings for work. It allows me to run a literary series with an open mic-that gives others, as well as myself, something to look forward to every Friday. This year has been described as the worst by many, but I still have a lot of gratitude.

GRATITUDE LIST FOR NOVEMBER 2019-2020

1. For my family, who mobilized as a team that has worked together for years, and for having the skills to work together through my mother's death and my father's illness. I cannot put into words the amount of gratitude I have for my family, especially for my brother and his family who daily take care of my father.

2. For my children, who turned out as well as any parent could hope. The decisions they have made are responsible and realistic. I have learned a lot about living life from being their father.

3. Spending the last six weeks of my mother's life daily with her was something I'll always be grateful for. I appreciate the people I work with, especially my supervisor, Eric S., and Area Director, Joan T., for allowing me time to do this without pressure to return. I am grateful that my good overall health, helped me be able to accumulate sick time. State policies for time-off in crisis situations proved essential.

4. For continued health in 2020, and for those who have done what they must to keep others safe. Without others' sacrifices, I may have become sick, but as of now, I am healthy, and have avoided Covid-19.

5. For Sarah, who has had her own situations to walk through, yet continues to give me support and joy. (also for her influence in my discovery of Bon Iver).

6. I have gratitude for my writing groups and that I continue to write, and am grateful for those who still find what I write worthy of being published.

7. I am grateful for enough life experiences to produce this book.

8. For a home that I love. It makes staying home easier.

9. For a job I enjoy.

10. For food to eat.

11. For my pets.

Lastly but most important--because, without this, I might not have nothing on this list:

12. I am forever grateful for the people who helped me to get sober ten years ago. Today, it's the people who help me to stay sober and teach me through their experience, strength and hope who help me continue my journey. I have been shown a spiritual Higher Power which is no longer myself. I have people, MY people, whom I talk to every day. I have learned to experience and live life today like I've never done before because of them. They have taught me humility, when before I didn't even know what that word meant. They have made me a better person. I love so many of them, very much. Each year is better than the last regarding my sense of true-self and my ability to love. I thank them for the last ten years.

Charles Timothy Gager,
November, 2020

TIMOTHY GAGER
2 0 2 0 POEMS

Table of Contents

Near Leaves and Light, co-written with Marguerite Gager   13

20/20 Scenes (as seen) Inside a Pandemic
    Jake's Narration after *I'm Thinking of Ending Things*   17
    To a tree cut Down   18
    Living with Rabbits   19
    Shadows   20
    Shelter   21
    Seclusion   22
    Social Distancing of a Town: Population 10   23

Strange New World
    Today's Daily Feed   27
    On Energy Drinks   28
    Whiskey India Delta Echo . . .   30
    June 10, 1960/June 10, 2020   31
    Nine Lives   32
    21 Lines / 2020 / Covid 19   34
    Guesses From a Stable Genius   35

Years…More Years
    Existential Crisis   39
    Holes   40
    Kleptoparasitic   41
    How Lucia Joyce was Treated   42
    Dark Tunnels   44
    Unformed Relief   46
    reply to someone who said
        you should write a poem about her   47
    November 2020, one year after, *I wish I was Here*   48

Leaps

    Bon Iver on Your Birthday   51
    When You Have This Connection   52
    Life's Canvas   54
    Motel Room   55
    Lemons   56
    Your Box of *Hot Cinnamon Sunset*   58
    Midwinter Aficionado   59
    Long Distance Thinking   60
    For Summer Lovers   61
    Unwritten Rules of the Situation   62
    A Few Days in the Berkshires *after Mass Moca*   63
    The opposite of Lightning in a Bottle   64

Travels Outside (of) My State (of mind)

    New York Confession   67
    Spin the Battle   68
    Ballet of Surrender   70
    Waking on Mt. Greylock *before sunrise*   71
    What You Should Do When Attacked by Bees   72
    Rosebud Winter   74
    Ocean Hotel   75

Near Leaves and Light

Even the leaves were threatening.
The orange ones especially.
When she saw, she shivered,
felt as if she could pluck
the light from the branches.

The noise, deafening.
think about this, think about this.
Thoughts more important than words.
In those thoughts, God is very near.
Then, there was singing.

~ Marguerite and Timothy Gager, 11/21/19

20/20 Scenes (as seen) Inside a Pandemic

Jake's Narration
after *I'm Thinking of Ending Things*

I create empty space
as snow falls.

I broom away
the best times
to forget to
distort the truth.

She's in my car,
super-sexy-someone-so
not in my car
in a suicide of snow,
obsession in the car
existing, alive.

I swear she's there,
well-read, re-played,
watching me feed mother
as she lay dying
after living forever
my father stopped

to remember this
is my life's work,
in their house to myself;
to paint, read in, release

what I have done.
What *have* I done?

To a tree cut Down

You can no longer grow, your roots bore into pipe
below a basic foundation under my neighbor's house.
They watched each branch cut, streamlined, and then saw
rope used to pull you down, as if you were nothing.

I will stand with the tree, protest going down.
Hope the structure can plumb itself,
become an element of change,
not just leafed branches severed,

raining down your splendor,
becoming dank down
To your trunk: Your appendages exposed,
cut up, taken away, forgotten.

Living with Rabbits

A woman once decided to visit
thought it *safe*, I live with rabbits
not preferring women.
Certainly not men, either.

I speak
to rabbits in
quarantine, or no one
else in the world.

Today I sing them songs
about what they are doing
with their lives, as they sleep
and munch hay into mulch,

And Rabbits boast long back legs
quite strong. they leap forward
great distances with a single push
they move quick-- short bursts,

good for leaping into the air or
forward over the ground,
when out of their cages,
I relate

sometimes…I do too.

Shadows

the dark day
becoming impaired
dark flint rendered hopeless
by cold, damp, air

the Sun goes down, fades,
creeps througH my room
sAturatethes circles round my eyes,
aDvancing contrast, as shadows under my chin
becOme the night sky
and the Weighted curtains
over my head descend, uselesS

Shelter

Remember, sunshine smacking
away the ugly greys
the everyday ways life is difficult.
Even cotton sheets
stubbornly refuse
to soften, hung on the line.

We'll never confess
we do not wash linen
after someone stays over–
the-sun not given permission
to bleach their lovers away,
but a sky can turn yellow, quickly,

then we shelter safe,
wishing to turn tornados back
into our nirvanas,
only to hide behind the rakes
standing upright
in the basement.

Seclusion

We touch each other.
Desire. Lives rapidly circulating.
Going viral—how we used to connect/

/we disconnect, in houses
cold media, we wish to touch
each other//   //being alone

this is the worst thing yet to
be the worst thing yet.
Still, there's contact.

How we touch each other
under the covers
is different today.

Pictures of primrose
are not real primrose.
Even the words die,

they can't hide.
We will not///
///bury them.

Social Distancing of a Town: Population 10

The highway is now covered in dirt
putting a halt to congregations,

driving. or gathering in Centralia,
to cease the morbid attraction,

a burning desire for people
to keep meeting in groups.

It was a death sentence, the town
a ghost, fire red-hot underground

drove out the residents, a populace change
from ten heel-diggers. to graffiti-artist tourists,

large crowds to be dampened
and safer to snuff them out—

another casualty of the virus, when
forcing an abandoned town to remain

abandoned—there's no evidence of embers,
again, a deserted town requires desertion.

Strange New World

Today's Daily Feed

She takes the same picture every day
making up for lost time
not finding a way out of darkness
or hiding behind wind walls for safety.

She wishes the world designated a screaming room,
the simulation revealing itself again, then
puts on a Bangles playlist at the mocktail reception
featuring a lavender lemonade and a mint mule.

She takes a picture of a used coffee filter
to avoid depression, the same each day,
but dancing delays this, as toking
marijuana suspends aging brains

Then, overheard conversations
in the cereal aisle in the supermarket
I visualize subtitles in their voices
shut them off if you want to

On Energy Drinks

Venom energy plus mango
Red Bull gored a mistake
Five Hour Energy if it takes
Rock Star to party like The Who
What, Where, a dude
can down a Shark
Adrenline Shoc,
ENERGY THAT'S not SMART
spelling it, S-H-O-C, lost a K
if you want to push a train, climb a peak,
seek Xyience to gain that "X"
by lose the "S"
3-D formerly U-p, lost the U and the P
and Amp, by Mountain Dew, by Pepsi
is speed too, without jug-swilling
hillbilly that are gun- silly
measures of currents
which could S-H-O-C-K you, Monster,
which is just that, but does it make you that?
And is B-a-w-l-s a crying fuel
or balling fuel?
Maybe for multi-tasking you
hoping it is
the "healthy drink."
 Zipfizz you mix in water, but stinks
of Kool-Aid, or Funny Faced, Goofy Fucking Grape
now we are gaining
Speed, Full Throttle, Restless,

Sparks Nos Spike Starbucks Bang Shooter
Redline Flatline Supreme
Meth Cytosport Kill Cliff Tropocool Ignite
Down the Sambazon Organic Amazon
Crack and Burn with Maurten Gel.
Hell, it's only time,
for time to fly.
Now you get to fly by time.
Now, you get time to fly, in fly-time.
Time flies. Fly there?
There…there.

Whiskey India Delta Echo . . .

    Linked coast, you've handled
      Over guarded lines, a ham radio
        Veteran, listening carefully, waves received,
          Emitted, picked up through static

        Yet, no mistaking that it is night
        Or far away you are reaching
          Usually evidence reveals itself

          Some manmade interference
          Originally receives a bravo
            Making the keying defective, but
          Useless, i am ready, i am
              Completely an amateur operator
            Heaven undecipherable.

June 10, 1960/June 10, 2020

Life was simpler when gushed
over a 1958 Norman Rockwell.
A policeman consumes Today's Special.
A boy-a runs away, thank God, he likes pie.
The cops only corrupt for eating on the job.

We've not moved much since another Rockwell
in an incident at a Arlington, Virginia lunch counter
when a different portrait was painted,
the runaway sitting was a Diamond, Dion, roughly
taunted, spit at, cigarettes tossed at, shots fired outside.

Sixty years ago exactly, the picture unmoving
when we stand up—in 2020 we still are sitting
at the counter in 1960, only proving to be a metaphor
in time, never serving a purpose protesting the way
things are/were/are—we are viewing huskers
with blu-ray specs gas-light blasts that cause our weeping.

Nine Lives

                    Cats really don't have them
             as all it can take is a house fire
                         maybe, some cat virus
                     no one will recognize

      or
     that
   sadistic
     son-
      of-
    bitch

             torturing a feral and postering on
YouTube: the fun cats, cute cats, kittens
                  falling into fish tanks, a lot
                 of lives lost in a cold stream.

Yet, a proverb: three he plays, three he strays,
   the last three he stays, mainly not known
          cats were so beloved in Egypt
        Goddess Bastet was depicted as half
feline, which is an absolute ball of fur,
            using history, science, and math—
which gives her only four and one half lives.
       So, be gone with all these thoughts
   Even Mercutio knew Tybalt had only one.

As their agility and flexibility raises
their reputation for reincarnation,
the truth is they never die more than once,
unless baby kittens on the internet are
covertly two-hundred year old reborn souls.
Nine—the number based the trinity of trinities?
Will it be honored nine times for Mr. Fluff's ritual
morning leap, from floor to the back of my head?

21 Lines / 2020 / Covid 19

First 1—person spread to another person in Hubei,
today 2—house cats tested positive,
and 3—bodies were found dead in same hotel.
The 4—main groupings: alpha, beta, gamma, and delta
with 5—key steps to stop the spread amongst footballers
6—feet of distance (unless it's ten feet, if people are running)
7—trillion dollars in global bailouts
with 8—corona related scams, beware
of 9—from a church in Harlem gone, the news reported,
Stephon Marbury found 10—million-masks in China
11—Alive.com would like to send you push notifications
Regarding the 12 hundred dollar checks—in the mail?
But 13—deaths a day at a New York Hospital
a pregnant mother's baby, 14 weeks early, flew out,
as the airline industry, had 15 deaths the past nine weeks.
A 16—year-old who was healthy, died in France
17—corpses were found in a shed, re-named a morgue
after being sick 18 days, the average length of Covid-
19—for really ill people, will never return
20—million dollars Ruth's Chris Steakhouse collected on
the 21st—of April, CDC says, the second wave will be worse.

Guesses From a Stable Genius

Supposing we hit the body
with very powerful light,

ultraviolet that hasn't
been checked.

Supposing you brought the light
through the skin or in some way,

you're going to test it
inside the body.

Supposing there's a disinfectant,
that knocks it out in one minute,

something by injection,
almost a cleaning.

Supposing you see it get there,
doing a number on the lungs.

It'd be interesting to check
the way it goes after one minute.

Supposing, that's pretty powerful,
the whole concept of the light.

Years...More Years

Existential Crisis

Hitting a snooze button—
an archaic term, like hanging up or
alack, alee, alow, amain, anent, anon,
freaking-A, Lord, gramercy.

Torturing the dog in order
to trim his nails,
buying and applying eye cream,
writing vomit—describing cat shit

to my wife, contributing nothing
to anything—but what it is worth
contributing to? The Salvation Army, maybe,
I'm angry over the dangling preposition

like ringing a bell, having one's bell rung,
causing alarm with ample confusion,
over mass confusion…of causation,
certes, clepe, eft, egads, e.e.…

Holes

In the end, there are always holes.
Why can't anything wrap up neatly?

Approximately virtual,
never fluvial, washed

away, rather than formed.
Maybe the storm's surge

is too strong, turbulent…
Note: who was the builder?

Who had stayed stagnant and why
the third choice wasn't considered?

No need for rosin and lampblack,
once the dust had settled.

We would again refuse discussion
while I dreamt of prelection,

lecturing anybody who'll hear
on the evidence of the consortium,

as a sinkhole opened a whirlpool
under the place I stood,

quick, afloat for one
second, I raised up my arms.

Kleptoparasitic

Going to heaven, tears
held back, snared,
in hell,

like a fly in a strip, stuck,
a glue tape restrictive,
morphine-like soaring

into the ProZap or skipping Prozac.
The limbo of an insect's life is
a human antonym, perhaps a hymn

of yang and yin, stuck within
majesty of dewdrops,
web affixed, holding

a place. On Earth,
unlike the Theridiidae, we beg
to hold the dying.

How Lucia Joyce was Treated

There are no structured steps
when a coryphée is dismissed,
the staged mind is darkened.

Reject the limitations
movements derived
from interpretation of feelings.

Rhythms become more fitful,
food thrown up—heaved
a chair at Nora on father's fiftieth.

Fires were set after Ulysses
cut phone chords
disconnect congratulations.

Jung felt she severed from reality,
while James had anogsognosia,
rubbed in the assessor's nose,

stated they dove in the ocean
to gather improbable creatures,
except James twirled to the surface,

while Lucia spun all the way down,
mouth openly giving in surrender
to unwilling incarceration.

James swam functionally as a genius,
cement-shoed dance partner,
all his weight tied to Lucia.

Dark Tunnels

Knew nothing about tunnels except
tubes   /   rocks   /   air-compression

yet, more worried about hidden leaks,
water pouring in, encompassing instantly

not buoyant cars, cannot drive to the surface
of anything—panicked, prayed,

struggling to end thanatophobia,
murky channels working overtime.

The child I left the house,
anxiety sitting as a passenger.

yearning to be on soil,
simple ground of home.

Yards' blades of grass,
brushed our heels, sinking

into soft dirt soul of
a mole's finished work.

We all stomped hills
flat, vying to hide

imperfections in the sod,
as if they never existed.

Even a tiny blind mammal creates
routes only they can see—*tunnel vision*,

(a pun of amusement parked itself,
such driving humor saved my life)

the painful wait for welcoming
light; annulling blind passages.

Unformed Relief

I took three pills
but they were antibiotics.

I saw my mother stare out vacantly
from a hospital bed, looking for St. Peter.

I overeat. I under eat.
I never eat

Anymore. Suggestions?
Treat yourself to self-care.

Do something
nice—call your father

who won't remember
losing his car keys

he doesn't remember /
looking for them for two days.

We took them (!) hid them.
Did we save a life?

Ride the haze of mercury,
know where to go.

We know where to go
Do you know where to go?
Tell me where to go.

reply to someone who said you should write a poem about her
~ for N.D.

I don't know if I can write this poem
The one about you, the one about…

I don't know—am I deserving of writing something
that's not right? I know, others can, if others can.

I can—pray, *please,* God, someone, write it
someone, God, worthy, or good enough,

but, not me, no, I can't. It's impossible.
You are gone, and it's impossible.

November 2020, one year after *I wish I was Here*

The furnace speaks for where I'm at today
I tell the man, the flame only stays on

a few seconds, and it's gone, like the sun.
Nighttime falls fast, then we all disappear.

It's the annual service needed, I recall,
going to church around a year or so ago,

the priest not talking of falling into darkness,
only toward the light, as that's where we all go

at that point, we all become tired, wanting to sleep forever.
It's not like tryptophan rather the late afternoon closing in

our eyelids, not heavy, just feeling like warm blankets
resting over our eyes. We must keep the covers on.

Leaps
~ for spg

Bon Iver on Your Birthday

Standing, felt harmony
filling me like music fills earbuds,
as if it were a matinee lasting till midnight.

I nearly toppled down the aisle,
floored by the moment.
Us, reaching a ceiling

I'm still not over—the wall
we scratch at—the surface
we pound with unannounced embraces.

The synthesizers bursting through stage lights,
like leaves blasted golden by sun streams,
the autumn's impetus hanging on us.

When You Have This Connection

It's like the kitchen is on fire,
when before you only smelled smoke.

you will buy, what you buy, food,
when you buy, if it's what she wants.

You will scrub the house clean
if she were to drop in. No need to call

when you didn't see her on *Wednesday*
as you've seen her the last three of those

like a pattern—a routine you had.
—like laundry on the same night, forever,

always on Wednesday,
the middle of the week.

But the day you sat her down, and confided
you had anxiety about all these changes, you said instead,

"the days are getting shorter, it's getting darker,"
You never liked losing those minutes of daylight.

"Spring always arrives" she answered
yet, I still mourn, like Whitman

his lilac blooming perennial,
and his drooping star in the west.

I love that she knows that verse,
and I love that she is right.

Life's Canvas

My heart was a red hibiscus
the day it blossomed for you

a hibiscus, like a kiss,
the red of its lips turn

like laughter, when considering
the Robert Burns painting—

an easy road, the canvas with
sunflowers parting, like a church aisle.

You walked with a bouquet of wild flowers
plucked from the random splattering of acrylic,

forever the Androsace Villosa's
eyes beautiful, pink.

Motel Room

key where we meet
flickers in the lock.
your eyes blink, snap
to say, "why do this?"

we leave
compassionate
cheap

Lemons

I do not carve a lemon
Make art on the side of a plate—
lemon crowns, or ducks, like the chef
Pépin making a big pig…bon apetite

I am not Martha Stewart or
my god, Stewart Martyr,
the little plumes or textures did
not make the banquets beautiful.

I will not ever suck a lemon
to make my face go sour but
I fed your dog one, and said
this is the food off my table

When I want to go elegant
I cut a slit into a slice, rest it
on the side of my glass
never toughing my lips.

I do not receive the lemon
to have the items to make
lemonade that way. Funny saying,
"orange you glad I…"

do not compare to a lemon,
in countless ways, my life,
is not like disasters, not like
pulpy, coarse, acrid, citrusy

lumps of a beast burning
my stomach linings, with others
paining to explain the refrain
of the failures in life as garnish.

Your Box of HoT Cinnamon Sunset

We sipped Harney & Sons
tea by a fire, spooned
unique and uncommon,

like the box said, "keep
without light, moisture,
scent, all tightly sealed."

Remarkably assertive,
the wolf-like flames
leapt and snapped.

Midwinter Aficionado

raced to daybreak
my dear, crossing
beau jesting, surely

our dice came up
how I roll.
snake . . eyes

So cold today.

It is ALL faunas here;
a chicken fowls out
the bile of connubial,

the times you pecked,
the times you saw trees
swaying, the woodpecker's sound

..-..-..-..-..-..-..-..- ..-..- ..-..-

        never fail,
at the point of staccato.

Long Distance Thinking

Loneliness was the handcuff.
I wanted bright fireflies instead-

on-off-on-off-I-couldn't-get-off
the sofa, stuck like glue.

Bought an accordion to make loud bellowings,
gave up and left the large slinky, a toy in the corner.

My dog strays there while I'm not looking,
his tail never wagged quite right, failing

like a helicopter with a crooked rotor mast,
pull me up please, so, *I paused,* his paws pause,

I'd lost my mind half-way through this ride
halfway through my existence, focusing,

trying to picture,
other halves living.

For Summer Lovers

The storm door made that hissing sound
You waited for the crash—surface on surface—

Paralysis-BAM-then   Now, do you follow?
Stay? Leave? What? Sit

on a hot wicker chair, no drink
on the dusty glass table.

Neighbor strolling—says hello.
You wave in silence, hearing

mosquitos buzzing loud
close to your ear, Is it trouble

to tiptoe down the stairs
with moaning half-broken treads

near the middle of the block?
Her car is no longer parked.

Unwritten Rules of the Situation

We don't say words of affection, no matter
what we goddamn love—guidelines,
 rules, lines, emotive ties, and unties.
Outside the trees added leaves, the months fell off.
Now, sunlight peeks through the bare branches.

We miss with kisses, complete, incomplete,
driving our hearts into a large stakes, strong and solid.
The chambers bind around them grasping
around puncture wounds creating a seal.

When life happens—there is remoteness,
loss, we have no control, the powerlessness
of a winter bolt of lightning blowing a transformer.
Still there's a spark inside the outlet,
the switch turned on and off too quickly.

A Few Days in the Berkshires
after Mass Moca

It was a huge installation—
views strobed, total blackness,
then the fire pit ukulele
Turrelled in light and dark

view strobed, total blackness—
mountain air, stars
Turrelled light and dark
getting away, not getting out of

stars and mountain air—
alone we woodstoved the Inn
getting away, not getting out
broke danced on the floor of a hot tub

we alone, woodstoved the Inn—
hot like the bottom of a pie tin
broke danced on the floor of a hot tub
yelled TIME, when time came today,

views of strobed versus total blackness—
the fire pit ukulele
Turrelled in light and dark
like it was a huge installation

The opposite of Lightning in a Bottle

is
*jolt-nope-not-going-
nowhere*
                         Jacuzzi,

a slow bubbling open
fluid system, nothing to catch

maybe a little cold when rising
from rock bottom—warmth

bubbling over, cordially rolling
off your skin

Travels Outside (of) My State (of mind)

New York Confession

New York was hard to find
only if I peeled the onion,
I can pray for sleep to overtake

a stumble, into place
and stumble out, never saw
what's in front of my face:

Life's jugglers, clowns, the beat
masters of three card monte, I
won until the stakes got higher

in a city of nightmares,
morning, afternoon, night
feel like different places
unless troubled, they merged
into one, I was awake through all
waiting for the city to let me go

forced to sing myself to supper
by climbing the highest mountains
the trees in The Village.

On 2nd street and Avenue C
I was lost, even with obvious
nomenclature of the corner

smack in the middle in the intersection,
my arms stretched out, Jesus,
4 AM, begging for crucifixion.

Spin the Battle

bottle spins
it'll land somewhere
on love?
it lands on drink
then I might lose
the handle
on that one
made it swirl better
the size and shape
might be impossible
it's a large problem
I am just not strong
it's very heavy
to spin again
I just want to make out
no matter how it turns
points to me
again the liquid
in the light
looks like green yellow
diamonds reflecting
red spiraling conclusions
so beautiful when lit

pick me, pick me, pick me,
until the last ugly one
releases an evil twist
don't pick me
say quivering lips
of those in the game
not able to stop it

Ballet of Surrender

Dancing, to get up
high, on my toes,
now pointe to each other,
hypothetical anonymity.

High, on my toes,
no one is looking
hypothetical anonymity
I kiss the ground I once fell on.

No one is looking,
now pointe, to each other,
no longer presumed difficult.
Dancing, I am up,

I kiss the ground I once fell on,
no longer presumed punished,
pirouetting won't turn to bellicose
feelings of uselessness, self-pity.

I no longer presumed punished.
I never felt I could be a ballerina,
feelings of uselessness, self-pity,
turn to rejoicing in these basements.

I never felt I could be a ballerino
pirouetting, can't turn to bellicose,
go rejoice in these basements.
I kissed the ground I fell on.

Waking on Mt. Greylock
before sunrise

Yellow, orange, red
streaked words kiss
our mouths have stars.

The cold mountains,
tell us, cope / look up
crisp skies. Early

breath evident.
lips-to-night,
became entangled

seriatim composing
discourse of shadowed
trees, still are the evergreens.

What you Should Do When Attacked by Bees

Run.
People make mistakes

standing, swatting, giving extra
time for the colony to recruit

when confronted by stinging bees.
Run.

Through shrubs or brush…
distract them.

Run.
Until they are left behind.

Some chase for
half-a-mile,

Don't be fooled
into water,

a poor shelter, every time
you come up, they

cover you, sting faces and noses,
no way to breathe.

Remember. Run.
Bees aren't being mean,

in a human sense
they just take exception.

Rosebud Winter

Late snowfalls on the Sangre de Christo
are confetti twirls in a tube, the sprinkle

erupts—builds blankets of white, a
frosting over emerald, never less green,

not everlasting than springtime's coming.
When her flowers are tricked, buried too soon,

they will now wait for water
to trickle down from her peak.

Ocean Hotel

Outside a window, the ocean
laps over rocks.
laps over rocks.
laps over rocks.

The foam is in the mixer,
a quick plop—resonates,
followed by fierce, violent, smacks
into rock wall, where a seagull sits
over the sounds, almost staged,
unmoved, a witness to this.
The sun opens early today,
6 AM when my eyes do not catch much,
eyelids inching up, like the water

rising outside a window, the ocean,
laps over rocks.
laps over rocks.
laps over rocks.

ABOUT THE AUTHOR

Timothy Gager is the author of sixteen books of fiction and poetry. He has had over 600 works of fiction and poetry published, of which sixteen have been nominated for the Pushcart Prize, and his work has been read on National Public Radio. Timothy has been nominated for a Massachusetts Book Award, The Best of the Web Award, The Best Small Fictions Anthology.

Timothy is the Fiction Editor of *The Wilderness House Literary Review*, and the founding co-editor of *The Heat City Literary Review*. Timothy has hosted The Dire Literary Series and now the Virtual Fridays Dire Literary Series since 2001.

ABOUT THE ARTIST

"*2020* was designed to represent how distanced and orderly humanity had to be in order to remain healthy and alive. In line, yet apart—yearning to be reunited once more."

~ Matt Siditsky
Art Director/Filmmaker

www.ingramcontent.com/pod-product-compliance
Lightning Source LLC
Chambersburg PA
CBHW031212090426
42736CB00009B/883